BOOK
TRAVELLER

BOOK
TRAVELLER

Bruce Bliven, Jr.

DODD, MEAD
& COMPANY
New York

First published in book form 1975

The material in this book originally appeared
in *The New Yorker*, and is published by courtesy
of The New Yorker Magazine, Inc.

ISBN: 0-396-06951-7
Library of Congress Catalog Card Number: 74-97
Printed in the United States of America

To the subject of this book,
GEORGE F. SCHEER

BOOK
TRAVELLER

There are about

two hundred American firms that publish what are called "trade books"—not textbooks or reference books but fiction, poetry, drama, biography, belles lettres, history, philosophy, books on contemporary affairs, children's books, and books that may not fit into any of those categories but also are meant to be read by literate people who like to *read* books. Not all trade books are literature, but every book that is or that aspires to be literature—as are, say, "Sense and Sensibility," "Alice in Wonderland," and "The Decline and Fall of the Roman Empire"—is a trade book. With uncharacteristic unanimity, trade-book publishers agree on the overriding importance of one question: How is one to transfer finished books from the warehouse to the hands of book buyers—people interested enough and affluent enough to pay for them? The trade-book publishers confront other serious problems: the cost of printing and binding books (either in hardcover or what are known as "quality paperback" editions) keeps getting higher; topnotch editors are scarce; authors have no more respect for deadlines than they ever had; and book reviews and free publicity for books are harder to come by than they once were. Still, book distribution seems more baffling than any of these.

Trade-book publishing is a small specialty in an industry that itself is not very big. In 1972, the wholesale value of all the books of all kinds that were sold in this country was a little more than three billion dollars. Even though this sum was twice as much as the book publishers had received a decade earlier, the sales of the book-publishing industry as a whole were nevertheless only slightly more than the sales of one soap company, Procter & Gamble. And three-quarters of the money was earned by books that were not trade books. Thirty per cent came from the sale of, among other items, textbooks and standardized tests in book form (nine hundred million dollars); twenty per cent came from encyclopedias and other subscription reference books, mostly sold door to door (six hundred and six million dollars); twelve per cent was professional and technical books for lawyers, doctors, scientists, engineers, and others (three hundred and fifty million dollars); four per cent was Bibles and other religious books (a hundred and twenty-six million dollars); and mass-market paperbacks, which are counted separately from quality paperbacks because they are distributed differently, more or less like magazines, accounted for eight per cent (two hundred and fifty-three million dollars). Trade-book sales were about seven hundred and fifty million dollars, and something like three hundred and four million of this came in through the book clubs. The remaining four hundred and forty-six million dollars covered sales of hardbound adult trade books, with a wholesale value of two hundred and forty-three million; quality paperbacks, worth fifty-five million; children's books retailing for a dollar or more, worth a hundred and twenty-eight million; and, finally, about twenty million dollars' worth of university-press books that were of general rather than specialized scholarly interest and were sold through trade channels. All of this represented the difficult part of book distribution. A good number of these sales were made to the country's libraries, but most of the books were sold to people through bookstores and the book departments of department stores.

The trade-book publishers' strong suit is variety. New tradebook titles—hardcover and quality paperback—average about twenty-seven thousand a year, or seventy-four a day. The *Times* gets nearly twenty thousand a year, or fifty-five a day, for review, although it cannot mention more than about twenty-five hundred. *Publishers Weekly*, the industry's trade magazine, divided the 1972 grand total of some thirty-eight thousand new books—new titles and new editions of old books, both paperback and hardbound—into twenty-three broad categories.

Books in the category that *Publishers Weekly* calls "sociology and economics," including texts and reference books, were by far the most numerous—more than sixty-four hundred. Adult fiction—thirty-two hundred—was second. Juveniles (fiction and nonfiction combined), science, and literature (essays, criticism, and literary works considered classics) were tied, at twenty-five hundred in each category. On down, in dwindling order, came biography, medicine, religion, and history, at fifteen hundred titles or more apiece; poetry and drama (which were lumped together), art, technology, education, philosophy and psychology (another combination), travel, and general works, all more than a thousand; sports and recreation, law, business, home economics, language, music, and agriculture (three hundred and ninety titles for the last). The number of new titles, omitting new editions, has been growing since the Depression, from seventy-five hundred in 1932 to twenty-six thousand four hundred in 1972, but that tremendous increase is mostly in the nonliterary categories, the leader being sociology and economics. New books of adult fiction—novels and short stories—were about as numerous then as they are now. Biography and poetry and drama are up, but by only a few hundred. Literature is up by more than eight hundred. And almost any trade publisher would admit that if he were to find a distinguished manuscript in any category—a candidate, let's say, for a National Book Award—he would not be certain that he could sell ten thousand copies of it.

Nobody I have

ever met knows or cares more about trade-book distribution than George Fabian Scheer, of Chapel Hill, North Carolina, who is not a publisher but a publisher's commissioned representative—a travelling book salesman. Scheer's territory is the South and Southwest, and he has been selling books there for twenty-eight years, calling on individual bookstores, the book departments of department stores, and book wholesalers, or "jobbers." Scheer has a reputation as a wizard among book salesmen, and his colleagues also consider him unusually knowledgeable about many other aspects of publishing—for good reason, since Scheer sees the industry from several points of view. Although, in the course of two major and several minor selling trips annually, he is on the road between Richmond, Virginia, and Amarillo, Texas, as many as twenty-two weeks a year, and preparations for his travels take up most of his time for four or five months, and although when he isn't travelling he works for some hours every day as a liaison between publishers and booksellers, he is far from being just a book salesman. He is a historian (co-author, with Hugh F. Rankin, of "Rebels and Redcoats," a documentary account of the American Revolution), a writer of children's books ("Yankee Doodle Boy" and "Cherokee Animal Tales"), an editor (of the Meridian Documents of American History series, for World Publishing Company), and a book reviewer (for the old *Saturday Review*, the *Times Book Review*, and scholarly journals). Moreover, as a publishing consultant, he has advised, among others, the Child Study Association, Dow Jones & Company, the North Carolina Diabetes Association, the National Park Service, and the Smithsonian Institution. And he is a literary agent for a number of authors whose work especially interests him. Beyond his professional involvement with books, reading is Scheer's hobby. "I must admit that I have ruined myself as a serious reader," Scheer once said. "I have become a book-taster by force of circumstance, and I have to make a conscious effort to keep from rushing ahead—skimming, with too much curiosity, faster than I can read. I love to lose myself in a book—that's what I mean by 'serious' reading. But then I also enjoy mere tasting to an inordinate degree. I even get a thrill out of holding a well-made book in my hands, just from the way it feels. I suppose that explains how I got into all this to begin with."

I first met Scheer three years ago, in New York, at a meeting of the Society of American Historians, where I had a chance to tell him how much I liked "Private Yankee Doodle," a Revolutionary War memoir by Private Joseph

Plumb Martin, first published in 1830, which Scheer had edited and annotated for Little, Brown. Scheer is a compact man in his middle fifties, who stands up straight with his shoulders back. He has a full head of close-cut black hair, graying at the temples; a trim salt-and-pepper mustache; and a full face, with round cheeks that come close to dimpling when he smiles. He speaks slowly and thoughtfully, with a faint trace of a Virginia accent. His manner is an attractive mixture of courtliness and friendliness. Our talk turned to book sales—rather naturally, since the room was full of authors—and I soon realized that Scheer knew more about the subject than the average historian. During the discussion, he offered no panacea, but he did observe that the trade-book publishers' distribution problems would get worse unless they did something practical to help old-fashioned, but not necessarily musty, independent local bookstores. Scheer has an economic prejudice in favor of such stores, since they make up two-thirds of his three hundred accounts, which buy for more than four hundred outlets, but his interest is also literary, emotional, and personal. He sees that many stores are struggling to survive, and fears that if the personal bookstores disappear—leaving only mail-order (including the book clubs), the chain bookstores, the mass-market-paperback racks, the department stores, the coin-operated book-vending machines, and the damaged- and remaindered-book outlets—literary quality will suffer. It will be harder for people to find the kinds of books he likes to read. "I like both fiction and nonfiction, and I guess I am sort of a nut about American history. The books I most enjoy usually fail to make the best-seller lists," Scheer told me. "They are seldom book-club selections—not of the major book clubs, anyhow.

I really fear that if the personal bookstores diminish in size and number, the publishers will have to stop publishing what I like best. There will be no way to distribute a modest success—a book selling fewer than fifteen or twenty thousand copies. That is not enough to interest chain bookstores or department stores, which are both important to books of wide general appeal but try to concentrate, as far as they can, on fast-moving merchandise. You can't publish trade books for their library sales, which are not much more than ten per cent at best. Selling by mail, except on the vast scale of the big book clubs, is highly problematical. The personal bookstores are the only other way. Thank goodness they have not yet vanished. By some miracle, people—lots of them young people—keep on opening bookstores. You can almost take it for granted that the ventures are under-capitalized—that's the most common mistake. And most of these people are shocked to discover that running a bookstore is extremely hard work. However, if the bookseller does everything exactly as it should be done, and if the store is in the right place, it is possible for him to do moderately well. So I do not say that all is lost. But I have been watching booksellers, of all ages, for more than a quarter of a century, and I've seen that merely staying in business has steadily grown more difficult. The personal bookstore cannot thrive on bestsellers alone. It cannot do without them, but it has to go well beyond the best-seller lists, because it must attract what I call real book buyers. These are the people who buy books constantly for themselves—books they intend to read and keep. There are people who cannot imagine getting through life without a lot of books. They are like opera addicts, who will skip a meal rather than miss a good perfomance. They are quite different from occasional book buyers, who come in, once in a long while, to buy 'Jonathan Livingston Seagull,' because everybody is talking about it, or a cookbook, because its author has been interviewed on television that morning. Or a book to give as a present. Some people are happy to spend twenty-five dollars on an art book for Aunt Eliza for Christmas although they never spend a nickel on a book for themselves. The occasional buyer's money, of course, is as good as the real book buyer's, and there is scarcely a neighborhood where real book buyers alone could support a bookstore. Still, I am convinced that an independent bookstore cannot afford to alienate those hard-core readers. They are difficult and demanding, goodness knows. If one comes in for the first time and asks for Kafka's 'Complete Stories' and you don't have it, he may be willing to let you order it for him. If he comes in nine days later and asks for something else and you don't have *it*, he'll wonder why not, out loud. Booksellers often answer, 'I'm afraid we're sold out'—because they'd rather fib than admit they haven't ordered the book at all. Maybe the customer believes it, maybe not. Then, four days after that, he comes in for John Kenneth Galbraith's new book and you don't have it. Well, you have lost that customer—probably forever. What's the use, he thinks. This store is hopeless. It doesn't have any stock worth mentioning. And he will look for another place, even if you are the only bookstore for miles."

Scheer shook his head. "The right balance is hard to achieve. The bookstore must satisfy a number of separate groups of people, and what pleases one group may not interest the other groups. There will never be a way of making books uniformly acceptable, so a broad inventory is most important. And yet the bookseller, since he has a

16

limited amount of money to put into his stock, must also be able to guess what the whimsical, impulsive, occasional public for best-sellers is going to want large quantities of—and he has to make those guesses and order the books long before the public ever hears of them. Most bookstores are weeks away from the publishers' warehouses and cannot afford to wait until the answers are in. That's a hard job, when you think of the thousands of possibilities. How could you have anticipated 'Bury My Heart at Wounded Knee'?"

Scheer pointed out to me that running a bookstore in New York City is very different from running a bookstore in, say, San Antonio. "I don't mean that a New York City bookstore is easy," he said. "If it were, there would be many more bookstores in the city, and there would not be so many of them clustered in one ten-block stretch in midtown Manhattan. But New York booksellers are spoiled. The publishers are right around the corner. There are big jobbers right in New York. The stores can demand delivery the following day and get it. But there are a lot of stores that sell books—perhaps three thousand—outside Manhattan. There are quite a few new jobbers around the country, but still many of those stores consider themselves lucky if they get books within a month or six weeks."

I saw Scheer

in New York several times during the following couple of years, and then, at his suggestion, I joined him in New Orleans on one of his two major annual trips, to see what selling books was like. Scheer was well into his trip, having already covered Chapel Hill, Richmond, Nashville, and

17

Atlanta. He met me at the New Orleans International Airport at noon on a warm and brilliantly clear Sunday. He looked fresh and jaunty in a tan open-necked sports shirt and tan summer slacks. I could hardly believe him when he told me he had had only a few hours' sleep. He had been caught in a bad rainstorm the night before, on the road from Atlanta, he said, and made an unplanned stop for the night, and then rose at the crack of dawn to finish the drive to New Orleans before my plane landed. "It wasn't anything," Scheer assured me. "When you travel as much as I do, you *count* on surprise delays, and I am just glad I had sense enough to stop for the night. Anyhow, Sunday is not a selling day. I use Sundays to catch up on paperwork, and I attempt to arrange my itinerary so that the long drives fall on Sundays. I ought to finish up New Orleans by Tuesday night—or Wednesday morning at the latest. The sad truth is that New Orleans, which used to be a fairly good book town, has been deteriorating. It may come back. There are all sorts of plans for civic revival in the air—a lot of rebuilding and renewal. I hope so, of course. I remember when I could not get out of New Orleans in much less than four or five days."

We were approaching downtown New Orleans, driving down Tulane Avenue, and Scheer pulled in at a motel. "I hope this is going to be all right," he said. "I've never stayed here before. Most unusual, because as a rule I stay at the same motels year after year—unless they start to come apart, as sometimes happens. I don't need anything very luxurious, so I hardly ever stop at a 'resort' motel, where I would have to pay ten or fifteen dollars more for essentially the same room. I've stayed for a long time at a nice place not far from

18

the airport, but last trip the air-conditioner was broken, the plumbing was stuck, and there was nobody around who could fix anything, and I decided that that was enough." We checked in, after Scheer had looked over our rooms with a practiced eye and pronounced them sound. We partly unpacked the trunk of his car, a light-tan four-door Cadillac, taking out his suitcase and mine, a rotary address file, a portable electric typewriter, and his garment bag. We left his two big briefcases in the trunk.

The back seat and floor of the car were filled with cardboard cartons of what I later learned were bundles of publishers' catalogues with order forms tucked inside them. As a commission man, Scheer works for anywhere from eight to twelve different publishers at a time, and he sells more imprints than that, because some publishers distribute books for other houses. Since most of the big publishers have their own salaried salesmen, Scheer, like all other commission men, represents medium-sized and small houses. On this particular trip, he was selling for Hawthorn Books, Schocken Books, Horizon Press, Pitman Publishing Corporation, Stephen Greene Press, John F. Blair, Louisiana State University Press, Holiday House, Barre Publishers (which distributed for the Imprint Society and David R. Godine), and Henry Z. Walck, Inc. (which was then distributing for Bradbury Press)."If there's a big best-seller on any of the lists, I shall be surprised," Scheer said. "But I've got some good books—Hannah Senesh's 'Her Life and Diary,' Lanza del Vasto's 'Return to the Source,' Irving Howe's 'Decline of the New,' in paperback for the first time. I've got Harold Rosenberg's 'The De-definition of Art,' and a beautiful book of photographs, Edward S. Curtis's fabulous pictures of the North

19

American Indian. Godine has a splendid edition of Walt Whitman's 'Specimen Days.' There's B. Liddell Hart's 'Why Don't We Learn from History?'—I expect that may do well —and, from the L.S.U. Press, 'The Changing Politics of the South,' by William Havard. James Ahern, who used to be chief of police in New Haven, has written a thought-provoking book, 'Police in Trouble.' Naturally, I have more cookbooks, gardening books, and books on how to do everything—from investing in the stock market to making wine— than anything else. Some of them are excellent, if I do say so. I don't have much fiction this time. 'Another World,' by James Hanley, some science fiction, and—oh yes, a gothic novel called 'The House Called Edenhythe,' by Nancy Buckingham. I understand it is good, if you care for gothic novels.''

Instead of travelling on an expense account and driving an automobile owned or leased by a publisher, as a house salesman does, Scheer pays all his own expenses. His commission rates, which are more or less standard, vary from ten to twelve and a half per cent on sales to bookstores and book departments and from five to seven and a half per cent on sales to jobbers. Commissions are figured monthly on the total amounts of the bills that his publishers send out to his accounts: the books' list prices multiplied by the numbers of copies bought minus the buyers' discounts (which range from forty to forty-six per cent) minus the buyers' credits for books returned. That means that Scheer's monetary interest in the sale of one copy of a given book is slightly more than half that of the author. An author's royalties are usually from ten to twelve and a half or fifteen per cent of his book's retail price. On a ten-dollar book, which a bookstore buys for six dollars, the author is likely to get a dollar and

Scheer sixty cents. And, of course, Scheer, instead of having just one book, or perhaps a handful of books, going for him, has all the books in print of all his publishers as potential money-makers. However, Scheer's expenses are high. His territory is too big for him to handle alone; were he to call on all three hundred of his accounts, he would hardly get back to Chapel Hill from one sales trip in time to start out on the next, and he would seldom see his wife, Genevieve, or their twenty-one-year-old son, George. And so for the past nine years Scheer's expenses have included the salary and expenses of an associate, Roger Foushee, who calls on about half the accounts. Foushee, who is in his middle thirties, is black-haired and bearded. He was a political-science graduate student at the University of North Carolina when Scheer found him and put him to work. Now Foushee spends every available minute when he is not working for George Scheer Associates working for the liberal wing of the Democratic Party in North Carolina and participating in Chapel Hill's civic affairs. Scheer is teaching Foushee everything he knows about selling books, and Foushee is learning his lessons well.

Scheer looked at his wristwatch. "We have to have some lunch," he said. "You can't come to New Orleans and not eat, you know. It's immoral. Let's see, Sunday lunch. I know —we'll have the shrimp salad at the Pontchartrain Hotel. It's really good. New Orleans carries on about its food until you are ready to go out of your mind, but some of it is delicious. Just let me make a couple of telephone calls and we'll go. I'll see if I can get Tess Crager at her home. I love Tess. She has an amazing bookstore out in the Carrollton district, near Tulane University. It is called the Basement Book Shop, but

21

it isn't underground. It's in an old rickety frame building, formerly a butcher shop—a fabulous place. And Tess is a fabulous woman, a real book person. She reads everything that interests her and then she calls her charge-account customers and tells them what she has for them. They can come around and pick the books up or send their chauffeurs for them. I wouldn't want to be in New Orleans ten minutes without calling Tess."

Scheer made his calls—he got Mrs. Crager all right—and over the Pontchartrain shrimp salad, which was indeed excellent, he continued to brief me. "Roger attends all my publishers' sales conferences with me—they're mostly in New York, and bunched around early December and early June—and then we go back to Chapel Hill and do our preparatory work, which is the one part of selling books I seldom enjoy. We make up matching jacket-books—one for each of us. They are big ring binders, nearly as big as the biggest coffee-table book, and they are our prime selling tool, along with the publishers' catalogues for the upcoming season. We give each new title at least a page. Usually, we mount its dust jacket on a hinge, so the bookstore buyer can lift it up, read the flap copy, and look at the back of the jacket, too. We take one publisher after another, from front to back, and each publisher's books, within its section, are in the same order as the publisher's catalogue, so if the buyer feels like it he can follow along in the catalogues as we turn the pages of the jacket-book. So you can see how important a jacket is, even at this early stage. We sell with jackets, not books. We may carry one or two finished books as samples —or perhaps a dummy book with blank pages, or a few sample pages, if the physical format is a crucial part of the book

22

—but that's all. In the case of children's picture books, where the illustrations *are* crucial, we carry folded and gathered sheets—the book itself, unbound, with its jacket but without its board covers. Then Roger and I make up bundles of the catalogues, with order forms, and snap them together with a rubber band. That's a bigger job than you might imagine—three hundred bundles, and a couple of dozen extras, because you never know when you'll come across a new bookstore. It's physically tiring, but greatly preferable to trying to collate them at the last minute in a driving rain in a parking lot. When I load all my sales material into my car, the stuff weighs at least four hundred pounds."

The total driving distance around Scheer's territory—his route combined with Foushee's—is about twelve thousand miles. Scheer handles Chapel Hill, Richmond, Nashville, Atlanta, and New Orleans, and then he makes a giant loop covering Baton Rouge, Beaumont, Houston, San Antonio, Austin, Dallas, Fort Worth, Amarillo, Oklahoma City, Tulsa, Little Rock, and points in between. Foushee stays east of the Mississippi River, seeing everybody Scheer does not, and his farthest point from home is Key West, Florida. Together they cover twelve states (Virginia, North Carolina, South Carolina, Georgia, Florida, Arkansas, Alabama, Mississippi, Louisiana, Texas, Oklahoma, and Tennessee), with a combined population of fifty-two and a half million people —slightly more than a quarter of the nation. In this huge area, there are more than four hundred places to buy a book, but Scheer and Foushee do not call on all the chain bookstores—many of which have their books bought for them nationally, including most of the Doubleday, Brentano, Walden, B. Dalton, and Pickwick stores—or on some very small stores. In the matter of smallness, though, borderline cases worry Scheer; he prefers to err on the side of optimism. "I know that time is my capital, and I'm always a little behind schedule. But if I want to stop, I stop. Once, when I was just starting out, I remember, I stopped at a very small sporting-goods store in South Carolina, which kept a small shelf of sports and regional-interest titles. The proprietor—a terribly brusque old gentleman—immediately said, 'I don't need any more books. I have all that I can sell.' Well, in my eagerness I pressed him a little. He was adamant. After a minute or two, I zipped my briefcase closed and started to walk out. He was outraged. 'Where are you going?' he called after me. 'You don't need anything, so I'm on my way,' I said. 'Now, wait a minute, young fellow,' he said. 'I did not say that you couldn't sit here and drum me for a while.' I sat and drummed him for a while—it must have been forty-five minutes—and in the end he gave me a right good order."

Although Scheer's part of the South and Southwest, with twenty-five per cent of the nation's population, buys less than ten per cent of the trade books sold in the United States, he does not feel he travels in a cultural wasteland. "Sales per capita are not good, but I greatly prefer the territory to any other, and I've sold books in the East and the Midwest, too," he told me. "I guess most commission men, given a choice, would pick a territory that included New York, Los Angeles, or Chicago. Those territories are certainly the most remunerative. I think you have to go deeper than raw sales figures, and for me there are a lot of towns in the South and Southwest where bookselling is a pleasure. Houston, for instance, is a great book town, and it seems to get better every trip. Nashville and Atlanta are good. I like Richmond—that's an interesting town to sell. And San Antonio—I love working there. But, considering my territory from a strictly economic point of view, not my personal bias, coverage is exceedingly expensive—a man has to travel a long way to sell a book, and he consumes his profits as he goes. He literally eats them up in food—not to mention time, gasoline, automobile wear and tear, and motel accommodations. That bothers the publishers, and with reason. They cannot afford to ignore a potential ten per cent of their total trade sales—no one in any line of manufacturing could—but the trick is to realize those sales without spending too much money in the process." Scheer explained that a publisher with his own salesmen would have to commit himself to paying something like sixty thousand dollars a year in salaries and expenses for two men to cover the South and Southwest, so unless a house is selling six hundred thousand dollars' worth of books in the territory, commission-man representation, at ten per cent of *achieved* sales, is a bargain. "That gives me a degree of security," Scheer said. "Only a handful of publishers are selling that many trade books in my territory. I'm needed. In fact, I've worked for more than seventy different publishers, and though that sounds as if I hadn't done well, I've been fired only a few times. I've represented several houses for long stretches of time. For instance, I sold Holiday House on one of my earliest trips, and I've still got it. I've been with Hawthorn for many years, and with Walck since it began, fourteen years ago. I like to think, though—especially when one of my many sales managers is grumbling at me—that if I lose one publisher I can find another."

25

What Scheer likes best about his territory is the people he sells to. The buyers he calls on, many of whom are the owners of the bookstores, are his friends. He has known some of them for ten or fifteen years, or even the entire twenty-eight years he has been travelling. He can be sure of seeing them only two or three times a year, but he meets some a fourth time at the annual convention of the American Booksellers Association; some drop in on him if they are anywhere near Chapel Hill when he is at home; and he talks frequently to many of them on the telephone between trips. He has been with them in spirit, if not in person, through business crises, marriages, the birth of children and grandchildren, divorces, bankruptcies, and store expansions. Scheer is an emotional man, and his passion for books is second only to his pleasure in people.

Scheer's familiarity

with small-scale retailing started when he was young. His father, George Fabian Scheer, Sr., ran a small quality-jewelry store, which Scheer's grandfather had established in 1887, in downtown Richmond. George, Jr., the eldest of four children, was born in 1917, and he helped out in the store from the time he could be helpful. He became an expert on antique clocks—Scheer likes to boast that he is the only book salesman in the country who is a fully qualified clockmaker —but when he was a schoolboy his ambition was to be a newspaperman, like Douglas Southall Freeman, then the editor of the Richmond *News Leader*. And, indeed, Scheer's first published newspaper feature story was bought by Free-

26

man, and ran in the *News Leader*, when Scheer was sixteen. The transaction showed something about Scheer's natural talent for selling, because the piece was really a school composition, which had been given a C instead of the A that Scheer felt it deserved. He took it down to the *News Leader* office at four o'clock in the morning—knowing that that was when Freeman began his incredibly prolific days of editorial writing, history writing, and radio broadcasting—and handed it to Freeman in person. Freeman was impressed, bought the piece, and printed it the following day.

During the next five years, while Scheer was attending high school and the University of Richmond, he wrote and sold many more feature stories, mostly on local history, and illustrated some with photographs he took himself, but he was forced to change his career plans when his father died, in 1939. Scheer's mother was faced with the problem of supporting three younger children—Betty, who was fourteen; Julian, twelve; and Charles, eleven—so George, at twenty-two, became the breadwinner, going to work in the jewelry store full time. Scheer already believed in careful husbandry of time. (He had been impressed by a motto on Freeman's office wall, "Time is ireplaceable," partly because it was misspelled.) It might be possible, he thought, to write a biography in odd moments, and after he had closed the jewelry store for the night he did a research on Francis Marion, the American Revolutionary War guerrilla fighter known as the Swamp Fox. Scheer is still trying to find time to write the book. His research is complete, however, and one of the happy by-products of his study was meeting Miss Genevieve Yost, the librarian of Colonial Williamsburg, one Friday in 1940. Williamsburg owns a valuable collection of American

Revolutionary War material, and Miss Yost, seeing that Scheer was frantic to finish reading a stack of documents, was kind enough to keep the library open an extra hour. The least Scheer could do in appreciation was to drive Miss Yost home. Within a few months, they were engaged.

An old back injury made Scheer ineligible for the armed forces, but in 1944 he got a civilian job at Camp Lee, near Petersburg, Virginia, working in the Quartermaster General's Office. He wrote training and field manuals. (Two of his assignments were "Cooking Dehydrated Foods" and "The Loading of Special-Purpose Ten-Ton Vehicles for Transcontinental Rail Transportation.") He learned a lot about book—or, at least, manual—production, and, urged on by a soldier friend, he drove down to Chapel Hill as the war was ending to see if he could get a job with the University of North Carolina Press, then directed by W. T. Couch. En route, Miss Yost read aloud to him everything that Couch had written—for periodicals like the *American Scholar, Saturday Review*, and *Publishers Weekly*—on university-press management, and Scheer memorized much of it. Couch was astounded that a young field-manual author should have such a keen, intuitive grasp of the problems of a university press, but there was only one job open—salesman. Scheer had been thinking of a job as an editor. Still, he accepted, hoping that he would be able to switch over to the editorial side when something opened up. His starting salary was minuscule. Miss Yost found that she could get a job at the University of North Carolina library, and she took it. Assuming that by adding two salaries together they could survive, George and Genevieve were married, on April 20, 1945.

Couch did not believe in breaking in a new salesman

gently. He started Scheer off by sending him to New York, with no guidance except a list of buyers' names and addresses. "Listen to those people," Couch said. "Don't try to tell them anything. You'll learn more by listening than by talking, because they know quite a lot and you know very little." Scheer was insulted at the time; later on he realized that the advice was wise. The University of North Carolina Press had a reputation for publishing good trade books as well as academic works, and Scheer had almost no difficulty in getting to see the important buyers, including Joe Margolies, at Brentano's; Morris Axelrod, at Doubleday; Igor Kropotkin, at Scribner; Harold Williams, at the American News Company; and William Epstein, at Bookazine. "I am sure that I seemed unbelievably green, and annoyingly over-confident," Scheer recalls. "But they were tolerant. I *had* to listen to them. I did not know how many copies anybody was expected to buy. When they gave me the numbers, I wasn't sure whether I ought to be happy or sad."

Scheer's greenness led him to one triumph. On his second trip to New York, he called on Lewis Gannett, then the senior book reviewer for the *Herald Tribune*, and told him he thought Gannett had made a mistake in overlooking one of the press's books—"Mexican Village," by Josephina Niggli. Gannett seemed surprised at finding a book salesman in his office, but he did not seem angry. Scheer told Gannett, "Some of the major reviewers have said some marvellous things about it." (Scheer was thinking of major reviewers in Atlanta and Chapel Hill.) Gannett thought he had probably handed the book to his wife, Ruth, for a preliminary reading, and he said he would try to remember to ask her about it. Two weeks later, a rave review by Gannett appeared, ending with "In a year of notably little distinguished fiction, 'Mexican Village' shines like a scarlet cactus in the desert . . . The whole crop of 1945 best sellers seems thin and wan beside it." The sales of "Mexican Village," which had been slow, immediately picked up, and the book went on to do very well.

Not long afterward, Scheer won more celebrity than a fledging book salesman can expect, by writing an article about his own experiences, entitled "New Adventures Selling Books," for *Publishers Weekly*. The appearance of his piece made Scheer feel, for the first time, that he really was a book salesman rather than a bookish young man waiting for an editorial opening. By the spring of 1946, he had been promoted to sales-and-advertising manager of the press, and he had commission men working for him in the Northeast, the Middle West, and California. He himself handled the South and Southwest, and he also called on the major jobbers and some of the big accounts in the other territories. Having acquired some feel for the marketplace, Scheer had no intention of losing it by sitting behind a desk. Within a few years, the press's sales volume had more than tripled. Scheer was delighted with his job but uneasy because he needed more money than the press was paying him, so he persuaded North Carolina to let him represent the Princeton University Press and the University of Chicago Press, on commission, when he travelled. North Carolina continued to pay Scheer's travel expenses, and he paid North Carolina a percentage of his extra earnings. He added publishers to his list from time to time, until by 1952 he was representing five houses in addition to the University of North Carolina Press, and he could not help noticing that he might soon be paying his employer in percentages from his commissions almost as much as his employer was paying him in salary. The idea of quitting to become a commission man pure and simple tempted Scheer—he thought he might be able to earn more in less time, and conceivably get back to doing some writing—but going off the North Carolina payroll was a terrifying prospect to a child of the Depression. Scheer had bought some land in Chapel Hill and wanted to build a house there, because he and his wife, enchanted by the place, were sure they would like to live there permanently. He brooded over the decision, trying to summon the courage to quit, until Genevieve telephoned one afternoon to tell him that her doctor said she was pregnant. Scheer was ecstatic, and, with perfect reverse logic, he told his boss, Lambert Davis, who had by then become director of the press, that he would be leaving in thirty days.

There were times, especially during his first year as a self-employed commission man, when Scheer felt he had made a mistake. One big best-seller could have relieved his anxiety, but he had none. (Before long, he was to earn six thousand dollars in a month selling Boris Pasternak's "Doctor Zhivago" for Pantheon. "Salesmen sound crass, I know, because they talk so much about the 'blockbuster,' the 'really big book,' and the 'runaway best-seller,' " Scheer said to me once. "I suppose we are even worse than publishers. You have to remember that we are all a little desperate, because literature doesn't support itself. And then—a thought that has consoled me considerably—not all best-sellers are junk.") Scheer's morale was sustained through low moments because he was traveling with a veteran commission book salesman, Ed Jervis, of Greensboro, North Carolina, whose talent for making

31

money was legend. Scheer had met Jervis in a bookstore on one of his trips, and they liked each other immediately. They were complete opposites. It is unusual for commission men to travel together, since they must compete in every town for the same buyers' time and attention, but Scheer and Jervis overcame that conflict (they took turns going to stores first) as easily as they avoided arguing about politics (Scheer was a Republican, Jervis a Democrat). It was more important that Jervis liked to shave before he showered, while Scheer preferred to shower first. They made their last trip together in 1964, when Jervis, who still sells books in the South, stopped covering the Southwest. Jervis taught Scheer, by example, that a man could make a good living selling books with candor, and without ever urging a bookstore to order one book more than he thought it could sell. Scheer, himself a candid man, had hoped that selling would not require him to exaggerate or deceive; Jervis's success was proof it did not.

From the

Pontchartrain, Scheer and I drove northeast on St. Charles Avenue, toward the French Quarter. "There is a nice young fellow named Oscar Brisky down there," Scheer said. "He's struggling to get a bookstore going—second-hand books, mostly—and I don't think he wants to buy anything much, but I'd like to stop by just to say hello." As we rode along, Scheer continued to outline the elements of bookselling: "What Roger and I look for at the sales conferences, after the sales conferences, and sometimes, though I hate to admit it, for days after we have started to sell, is the proper 'handle' for each of the new books. We need a capsule description, the shorter the better, that puts the book in the most realistic light as far as potential bookstore sales are concerned. We hope that the sales conference will give it to us, ready-made—that the editor or the publisher or the sales manager, or whoever presents the book, will tell us what it is. He *tries* to. But I have attended more than five hundred sales conferences, and most of the time the salesmen are forced to work it out for themselves. We are not shy about asking for help. Time and time again, one of us interrupts to say, 'It's beautiful. I'm sure the book is as distinguished as you say. But what handle can we use?' Even experienced and sophisticated editors, sometimes, have not thought that far. Or they cannot envision what happens when the salesmen meet the bookstore buyers. 'Handle' is a blunt, philistine word—precisely why the salesmen use it. We are seldom expected to assign the book its rightful place in literature— although if you could honestly say, 'I've read the galleys, and this is the best book that has been written since the King James Bible,' that would be an excellent handle. Mostly, we need to explain why *this* cookbook, in the face of all the other cookbooks, deserves a place on the cookbook-collector's shelf. Or why this gothic novel is expected to sell even though the competition is so great."

Underselling is almost as bad as overselling, Scheer said, and a good handle protects the bookstore from ordering too few copies. It is also something that the bookseller can use, as long as the book is in stock, to explain to his customers why they ought to buy it. "Just to give you an example, I'm selling a book called 'Home Landscaping You Can Design Yourself,' by Irving Roberts." Scheer went on. "There are half a dozen do-it-yourself landscaping books. The reasonable question is: Why another? Well, the Roberts book is practical. He is an engineer, an important officer in a big company, and landscaping is his hobby. His approach to landscaping is precisely what you would expect. He doesn't waste any time describing the beauty of the azalea or the perfume of the honeysuckle. He gets right down to the working specifications. And there is the handle I have been using—'landscaping as a professional engineer would approach the subject.' That's why the book should sell, and the orders have been good."

Scheer spoke about the frustration a book salesman experiences when he has what he thinks is a good book but lacks an effective handle for it—when the publishing house is excited and the author is optimistic but the salesman is unable to get anything like the advance orders that the book deserves. "That's a nightmare," he said. "You *know* that your orders are too low, and you know it is your fault. Six months later, on your next trip, the buyers are going to accuse you of having slighted the book. A couple of years ago, when I was selling for Farrar, Straus & Giroux, that happened to a distinguished novel by a well-known author. As the first sales figures came in, they were absurdly low. It wasn't just me. *All* the salesmen were missing on the book, because none of us had the right handle. And Farrar, Straus—greatly to its credit—stopped us. The book was postponed a whole season, so the sales strategy could be rethought. The next time around, with the help of an expensive promotion piece—a special advance paperback edition, with a letter from the publisher as a front cover—the salesmen more than doubled the advance. But that is an unusual case."

We took a right on Canal Street, then a left onto Decatur Street, and continued northeast, past Jackson Square and the French Market. "After they have an idea of the book, most buyers want to know how much enthusiasm there is for it on the publisher's part," Scheer said. "How big a sale does the house anticipate? You hear so much about 'surprise best-sellers,' and then you see so much evidence, in the form of piles of remaindered books, of publishers' dashed hopes, that it is hard to realize that most publishers' predictions are reasonably accurate. The salesmen usually play a part in formulating such predictions. The initial print order is often not decided upon until the house gets their reactions. Somebody on the editorial staff, reviewing the sales conference, may say, 'I noticed that the salesmen didn't exactly catch fire. I wonder if we have been thinking too big.' The estimated advance sale, which is ordinarily broken down into a quota for each territory, may be reduced. Some publishers ask their salesmen to help set their own quotas. Bookstore buyers want to be clued in to the publisher's forecast, and the size of the first printing ordinarily tells the story. If it is big—fifteen thousand is big—I make a little note about that in the jacket-book. There is no need to tell the buyers that the publisher thinks a book's prospects are routine—in fact, it can be embarrassing. Let's say I have a first novel that the house adores. I love it, too, and I want to give it a good spread—that is, sell at least a few copies to as many of my accounts as will take it. Still, the first printing may be no more than five thousand copies—which is often correct for

35

a first novel. Even if we sell them all—every single copy that's left after the review copies and the complimentary copies have gone out—the advertising and promotion outlays for the book are going to be negligible. Not much more than a thousand dollars, probably, by almost any rule of thumb. Enough to buy a couple of modest ads."

Scheer went on to name some of the early indicators of success—selection by a major book club, an important sale of prepublication rights to a magazine, a movie sale, a paperback sale. "If anything of the sort has happened to one of my books, I do not suppress the news. But you have to keep the big-time blockbuster, and the publicity it engenders, in perspective. There are likely to be half a dozen a season—maybe twelve a year—and the chances are, to my regret, that I will not have one. Books do sell five hundred thousand copies, but I am concerned with alerting my accounts to any title that is going to sell, say, ten thousand. They should not pass it over. Roger and I ought to get an advance sale of at least six or seven hundred copies of such a book in the South and Southwest, which means we should average two or three copies everywhere we stop. If any unusual publicity has been arranged, I make a note of that, too, but I am selling so far ahead of the publication date that this seldom is a factor. Then, perhaps the author is a celebrity, talented at self-promotion, and a fifteen-city tour is being scheduled for him. I'd mention that, of course, if he was going to be within radio or television range of the bookstore's customers. Conceivably, the book has a good advance review or two. I would paste them into the jacket-book. In the case of the average book, the bookseller sells the book to the customer with little outside help. The customer learns the book exists when he comes upon it on the table reserved for new books, or when the proprietor of the shop mentions it: 'Did you notice that Wirt Williams has a new novel, "The Far Side"?' There are big and little bookstores, but even in a big one—say, Ted Brown's downtown store in Houston—the proprietor and the salespeople know many of their customers by name. In a small suburban shop, where most of the trade may be charge-account customers, a total stranger stopping in to buy a book can be a rarity. So when I get to Oklahoma City, four weeks from now, and offer a comprehensive history of American lighthouses, a bookstore buyer there will have a good idea of how many he can sell—he can very nearly name the customers. To make those sales, he must have a copy of the lighthouse book on hand when each of those prospective buyers comes in—the right stock at the right moment. Ultimately, a bookstore is what is within its four walls then and there. The buyer puts the stock there, and the quality of the store depends exactly on how well the buyer has bought. What I do is try to clarify the potential of my books for my buyers. I call it selling. It *is* selling, but it is a form of collaboration, too."

The building, on

Esplanade Avenue, near Bourbon Street, where Scheer expected to find Brisky's Old Mint Book Shop was vacant, but there was a sign in the otherwise empty window. "Marvellous!" Scheer said. "He's moved to Royal Street. I told him last year that he'd never make it here, and 1036 Royal Street is a much better location. He's still a little to the east of the mainstream of the tourist traffic, but I imagine it's a big improvement."

Brisky's new shop had an attractive sign and a quaint, bay-windowed façade, freshly painted white, but its interior was a letdown. The place was lined with second-hand books, as drab as only second-hand books can look. The display tables were card tables. There were only a dozen or so new books on two of them, and in the gloom their pristine dust jackets shone like jewels. I felt we were at a rummage sale rather than in a bookstore. Brisky, a slender, worried-looking man in his late twenties, wearing gray flannels and a tweed jacket, seemed discouraged. He said, "This is better, but it's still very slow. I am beginning to get a small number of fairly steady customers, and that encourages me. Mostly, I am attracting browsers, and I find I am working ridiculously long hours. I may decide to go back to school."

Brisky's spirits seemed to rise as he talked to Scheer, though Scheer said little. Mostly, he listened. He did remark that one could not expect too much too fast, he agreed with Brisky that running a bookstore was indeed hard work, and he reminded Brisky of a point he had made six months earlier: that the Old Mint Book Shop needed "a more sharply defined character" to make the browsers feel that it was an authentic part of the French Quarter. Brisky had said when we first came in that he was more interested in reducing his inventory than in increasing it, but before long he began to wonder what Scheer had to sell. Scheer had not brought any of his sales materials, but finally, at Brisky's request, he walked the half block to his parked car, returned with his jacket-book, and opened it out on one of the card tables. "I'm afraid I haven't got much for you," Scheer said, "but

38

we can flip through the book so you can see what there is."

That seemed to whet Brisky's appetite. Whenever Scheer flipped a page quickly, Brisky wanted to turn back to it—as if he suspected Scheer of concealing a book from him. Within half an hour, Brisky had ordered about twenty books—single copies, and two or three copies of about twelve titles—which would cost him perhaps fifty dollars at his forty-per-cent discount, and he seemed positively cheerful. Scheer left a bundle of catalogues and order forms, and three or four postage-paid self-addressed George Scheer Associates mailing labels. "Drop me a line if there's anything I can do," Scheer said. "And I'll stop by on my next trip."

That pleased Brisky, and I realized that Scheer's call had flattered him—it was a token both of interest and of faith. "Remember, it never pays to get discouraged too quickly," Scheer said to him as we left.

During the next two days, we had to rush to fit in all of Scheer's well-established accounts. Though I knew that we couldn't waste a minute—not if we were going to get to Baton Rouge before Tuesday midnight—Scheer relaxed with the buyers as if he had all the time in the world. In New Orleans, they were almost all women: Rhoda Faust, at the Maple Street Book Shop; Kay Archer, at the book department of Maison Blanche, a downtown department store; Suzanne Link, at Books Etc.; Zelda Soignier, at the Tulane Book Store; Florence Henderson, at the Catholic Book Store; and Tess Crager, at the Basement Book Shop. Except for Miss Faust, who had just taken over the Maple Street Book Shop from her mother, Scheer knew them well. He called them by their first names, and they called him George. All the stores except the Maison Blanche book department were in the Carrollton neighborhood, within a few blocks of one another. They were not far from the Tulane campus—and the Tulane Book Store was right on it—but I gathered that the Maple Street Book Shop, which had a lot of paperbacks that might have been "suggested further reading," was the only store besides the Tulane Book Store that was getting many college-student customers. Carrollton Avenue is a shopping and residential street that runs through several well-to-do neighborhoods. Books are luxuries, and bookshops go where the money is. The bookshops in the Carrollton area were attractive: though they were all small, with limited stock, each had a well-defined individual character. I thought how welcome any one of them would be in my section of the West Side of Manhattan, where hardcover books are difficult to come by. My favorite was Tess Crager's high-ceilinged place, which had a genial atmosphere of barely controlled clutter, its walls adorned with scores of old photographs of literary celebrities—such as Hendrik Willem van Loon, Gertrude Stein, Sinclair Lewis, W. H. Auden, Ogden Nash—who had visited the Basement Book Shop. It was clear to me, though, why Scheer was gloomy about New Orleans as a book town. We had called on a major part of the city's bookstores, omitting only a couple of chain bookstores and the book department of the D. H. Holmes department store, whose buyer was out of town, but none of the orders was anything to boast about. Their total value was perhaps twenty-five hundred dollars. Scheer may have earned two hundred and fifty dollars, but his expenses had offset a big part of it. He had not expected to do better, he said, but he was frank in admitting that the results depressed him. He hastened to add that it was not the buyers' fault. He felt they had ordered about as many books as they could sell, with an exception or two—for instance, they had resisted "Weep No More, My Lady," Mickey Deans' book, written with Ann Pinchot, about Judy Garland, although Scheer expected it would sell quite well. Whenever such an order seemed too small to Scheer, he spoke up. He told most of the buyers that he thought they were underestimating the size of the Judy Garland cult. Everyone responded, as if they had been conferring on the point, that they had been too enthusiastic about two earlier Judy Garland books; they were afraid of getting stuck again with copies they would have to return. At Scheer's urging, the buyers would order a few additional copies of a title, or agree to try a copy or two of a book they were inclined to pass up, but Scheer seldom put pressure on them, and when he did, it was never great. When they thought they could not sell a book, Scheer accepted their verdict. (A salesman who over-sells is, of course, confronted by every one of his errors, standing unsold on the bookstore's shelves, on his next trip.) Often, the order was Scheer's suggestion. "I don't know, George," the buyer would say. "How many do you think I need?"

"Three or four," Scheer would answer.

In that case, the number ordered would most likely be three.

But an order for three copies, which had sounded pathetic to me early on Monday morning, sounded pretty good by Tuesday night, because I had heard so many "two"s and "one"s, and even more "none"s. A five was heartwarming, a ten was excellent. There were only a few orders for fifteen copies, and they were mostly for backlist staples, like

Tasha Tudor's "First Prayers" for children, which had evidently been selling splendidly in both its Catholic and its Protestant editions.

I not only learned how hard it is to sell a hundred copies of a book at the rate of three of four per store, I saw how little time Scheer had to spend on any one title. He was selling two hundred and six new books—a hundred and fifty hardcovers and fifty-six paperbacks. (Among the latter, besides Irving Howe's book, were "Last Reflections on a War," by the late Bernard Fall, "What Black Politicians Are Saying," edited by Nathan Wright, Jr., "Maple-Sugaring," by Myrtie and Floyd Fellows, "Riddle Me This," by Frances Chrystie, and "On Judaism," by Martin Buber.) It was not an unusual number for him, or for any commission man, nor was it more than many house salesmen handle. Scheer had explained to me that a full-scale selling session took all morning or all afternoon, and that therefore he could take care of only two big accounts a day. But I had not figured out that the time from ten o'clock in the morning, which is when most book buyers begin buying, to one o'clock is only a hundred and eighty minutes. And Scheer had a lot to do besides describe the merits of the books. In every store but one—Scheer told me it was the case in nine out of ten of the stores he calls on—he had to improvise a place to work. Most of the stores had desks, but they were loaded with correspondence, catalogues, invoices, and directories, which had to be pushed aside. The buyers had worked with scores of salesmen during the previous weeks, and yet they were as unprepared for Scheer's call as if it were an event without precedent.

Then there was a lot to talk about before the selling

could begin. Scheer's mustache was new; he had had to grow it because he lost a bet with his son. It surprised everyone, and it had to be explained and evaluated. (The consensus was that it should stay.) The buyers wanted to know how Genevieve was, and whether his son, George, was liking his sophomore year at Brown University. Scheer, in turn, wanted to know about their families, and he passed along news of and regards from booksellers he had called on during the first part of his trip. And, invariably, the buyers wanted to tell Scheer that they felt that the publishers—all the publishers, not just the group Scheer was representing—were trying to drive them crazy. Some spoke angrily. Others sounded puzzled: "What in the world are they trying to *do* to us, George?" They all felt that inhuman forces were working against them, and all held the publishers responsible. Most of the illustrative stories had to do with books they had ordered that either had taken forever to arrive or had arrived all wrong or had arrived twice. There were complaints about errors in billing and errors in credits for returned books. The buyers were convinced that once an error had occurred it was well-nigh uncorrectable. They asked Scheer to explain why publishers need to keep revising their discount schedules. They said that keeping track of ever-changing terms and ever-changing credits for returned books was a full-time occupation in itself. And, they asked, why couldn't the publishers decide by the time the jacket was printed what the retail price of a book was to be? (Price changes that were announced after the booksellers had received the books meant that they had to paste new prices, on gummed labels, on the jacket flaps.) None of the buyers thought that Scheer could do much about the sins of

43

the publishers, except possibly those of the ones he was working for, and yet, knowing that he would be in New York before very long, talking to publishers, they spoke as if they felt he might convey their messages. Whenever a specific complaint was made about one of Scheer's publishers—an order unfilled, a shipment billed twice, a letter unanswered for weeks, or whatever—he got out a pocket memo pad and wrote it down. "Inexcusable," Scheer would say. "It's all too much for the damned computers, apparently, but I'll get on it right away."

There were frequent interruptions. Each buyer had at least one assistant clerking in the store, but as the authority on what was in stock or on order, each one, except Kay Archer, at Maison Blanche, had to stop to take phone calls. If two or three customers needed attention at one time, the buyer would leave to help wait on them; far from resenting this, Scheer helped out, too, on several occasions. After he had gone through a publisher's new books, he would spend quite a bit of time on that firm's backlist. (A book goes on the backlist the day it is published; some of the books he talked about were only a few weeks old.) In the aggregate, Scheer's backlists contained two thousand five hundred and fifteen books, four-fifths of them hardcover. He did not need to say much about them. The buyers knew which books had been selling well—they just needed to be reminded of their titles. Besides the lists at the back of the publishers' catalogues, and on the backlist order forms, Scheer had a visual aid for two publishers' books which was a sort of miniature of his jacket-book—several hundred three-by-five color photographs of backlist jackets mounted in a small ring binder. He flipped them over quickly, with only occasional comments, and the buyers recognized those they wanted. In many cases, backlist orders were larger than new-book orders, and Scheer had trouble at times writing down the numbers as fast as the buyers spoke them. From time to time, an inventory question would arise. "It's been selling, but I think we've still got several copies left," a buyer would say. "You sold me too many on your last trip, George."

The moment Scheer entered a store, he began studying the shelves, and every time he lost the buyer's attention, even momentarily, he studied them further. What was on display was approximately what was in stock, because, except for Maison Blanche, no one had much storage space. Scheer was often able to say authoritatively, "You're down to two. I just counted them. I think you can use another five." If he did not know how many copies were on hand, he got up, walked to the appropriate section, and looked. That some-times led to some shelf-straightening, and a few additional seconds' elapsed time. (Scheer hates to see the copies of one title scattered; it is axiomatic among booksellers that the more copies you have of a title the faster it moves.)

What with all the diversions and distractions, I esti-mated that Scheer spent only half his time selling his new titles. Many of them were disposed of in seconds. He would turn a page of the jacket-book and read a title, and before he could finish his handle the buyer would reject the book: "I think I'd better skip that one, George," or "Let's go on," or, sometimes, just plain "No." A fast negative was often accompanied by an apology: "I'm sure it's a good book, George, but there simply isn't any interest around here in art criticism." Most of the books called for some considera-tion. When a buyer knew on sight that she wanted to order some copies of a particular book but did not know how many, it took her a while to make up her mind. Scheer often suggested a number, but he never seemed to hurry the decision. He sounded willing to talk indefinitely about any title. I knew that if a buyer wanted to hear more, Scheer was prepared to say more, because he had at least sampled all the new books—except for a few he had not been able to get, even in galleys. He had read twenty or thirty with care, including some he had not liked at all. Scheer never says he likes a book he doesn't like; in that case, he simply doesn't bring up the fact that he has read it. If he is cornered, he tells the truth, and reminds the buyer, "But my personal reaction has no more to do with whether it will sell than yours will have." The buyers listened to Scheer, between interruptions, with close attention; they were hungry for information, and intent on visualizing the finished books from the evidence of the jackets. They often did reach out, as Scheer had anticipated, to feel the jackets and swing them on their hinges. (It would be much easier but less effective, Scheer feels, to mount the jackets in transparent plastic envelopes.) Although none of the buyers said so, I felt that, for all their seriousness, they were slightly disappointed. They looked forward to a number of his books, but they were hoping for something great that was sure to sell extremely well, and on this trip they did not find it.

Allowing for everything, Scheer was able to devote about ninety out of each hundred and eighty minutes to pure new-book selling—a little more than twenty-six seconds, on the average, for each of his two hundred and six new titles. There were a number of five-second or ten-second books, briefly described and quickly rejected. Still,

46

when Scheer did have his full say he spent about a minute on a book. I could not help thinking that that was all he would have for another "Moby Dick."

Tuesday night, on schedule, we were driving through a drizzle on Interstate 10, headed for Baton Rouge. Scheer said, "Now you understand why at one sales conference after another my voice is raised with my annoying question: 'Well and good, but what is the *handle*? What can I tell the buyers? I often think how shocked authors would be if they listened to the salesmen selling their books. They've worked for a year on their book—two years, three years, maybe longer. And there it is. A word or two and the decision is made. I am not selling faster than other salesmen; on the contrary, I am kidded about having too much to say. I don't think many authors could stand it."

And yet, Scheer said, he feels that the selling-buying process is less haphazard than an author might think. "Naturally, I seldom feel that I have done justice to the nuances of any real work of art," he said. "But I can usually look over my tally sheets at the end of a trip and see that I've achieved a reasonably good spread for it—let's say that two-thirds of my accounts have ordered at least a copy or two. The book has a chance, assuming that all the other salesmen have done about equally well. If two booksellers out of three have it on publication day, at least it is alive. Books *have* survived a wretched advance sale; that is, you can collect anecdotes, if you care to, about slow starters, ignored for a long time, that have gone on to good sales, even great sales. It happens, but it is very rare. I can almost never expect a good reorder on a second trip if I haven't had a good order on my first—not unless something truly extraordinary has happened

47

in the meantime: a National Book Award, a Pulitzer, or the Nobel Prize. Most good reorders represent the experience of the particular bookseller. A kind of momentum has developed. Say she took five initially. They disappeared fast, and she has no doubt that the store can sell five more, or even ten, because her customers are talking to each other about the book. A buyer for a small bookstore is in very close touch with that reality—although there are enough surprises every season to make life interesting. Don't be deceived by my buyers' politeness. They know almost instantly how many copies they can sell, and I doubt whether their estimates would improve much if they took ten times as long to buy. Fiction is harder to predict than nonfiction. If I am selling for a house that runs heavily to fiction, I know, and my accounts know, that the returns on that list are going to be high. Of course, there's an exception to every generalization about bookselling; ordinarily, it is hard to raise high expectations for nonfiction, whereas the mere mention of a famous novelist's name is exciting. But novels stall. The salesmen get out a good advance of thirty thousand, everything looks fine, and they follow up with ten thousand more. Unaccountably, the customers stop buying at twenty-eight thousand, and twelve thousand copies are headed right back to the publisher.

"Bookstore buyers are cautious because returns are a nightmare. The booksellers don't buy on consignment, as many people think. It is a real sale. They get credit for returns, but full credit is not easy to come by. The books must be in good condition, must be properly packed, and must be returned within a specified time. If the bookstore has mislaid the original invoice, some publishers assume that the store

48

got a bigger discount than it really did. Even under the best circumstances, the bookstore loses on returns, because it has to pay the return shipping costs, but a more substantial loss is all the paperwork and time involved. I hate to see the returns on the books I've sold get as high as fifteen per cent, although I understand that the national average for all publishers is nearly twenty per cent. Like all salesmen, I'm under constant pressure on this. If my returns are low, my publishers suspect me of underselling. If I sell too hard and returns are high, my accounts turn me off. It's a tightrope. Not every bookstore buyer is a genius, you understand. Some buyers just plain annoy me. My bête noire is the buyer who says, 'Oh, I see you have a new book about Taiwan. Have you seen Harper's new book about Indo-China?,' and proceeds to tell me all about Harper's new book. Still, my three hundred buyers buy wisely, in the aggregate. When I run into resistance on a title, I call Roger, and I find, almost invariably, that he is running into resistance, too. And I'm almost willing to bet that the East has been bad, the West has been bad, and the Middle West has been bad, too. The author, the publisher, and the salesmen have all been dreaming pipe dreams, and the bookstore buyers, in their collective wisdom, have brought us back to earth."

Business improved

as Scheer and I travelled west from New Orleans. Early Wednesday morning, he got an excellent order at Claitor's, a huge bookstore on the southern outskirts of Baton Rouge, in a building that looks like a factory. Actually, it is an adjunct of a publishing operation, where a man named Robert Claitor produces regional, technical, and legal books. It has half a dozen clerks, trimly dressed stockroom girls, and a vast selling area with bookshelves rising all around to a double-height ceiling. (The shelves that cannot be reached except by ladder are used for storage; there is also a big stockroom at the back of the store.) Sometimes Mrs. Claitor does the buying but she was away, and an assistant, Cecile Bourgeois, was taking her place. She was tidy and precise, and although she sometimes hesitated over a title, she knew exactly what Claitor's wanted. Almost every time Scheer turned to the next page in his jacket-book, Miss Bourgeois rolled her eyes heavenward, as if to say, "My goodness, what will they think of next?" She said hardly a word except "I'll take ten," or whatever the number was; she ordered some copies of almost every new title; and there was a sprinkling of twenty-fives among the numbers. There seemed to be an added spring to Scheer's step as we walked back to his car.

We went on to Melvin Shortess's small store, Shortess Paper Books—a misnomer, for perhaps a quarter of the stock was hardcover—in one of the blocks bordering Louisiana State University. Melvin and his wife, Helen, are among Scheer's oldest friends; he had taken them to dinner, after drinks at their home, a handsome house in the suburbs, the night before. Until a few years ago, the Shortesses ran a much larger bookstore downtown, in the main business district of Baton Rouge. They regard Shortess Paper Books, about a mile from where they live, and hardly more than twenty feet wide and thirty feet deep, as semi-retirement; they can run the whole business by themselves, working six days a week. Selling at Shortess Paper Books took Scheer no more than an hour. Shortess wanted quite a few titles—his customers are mostly university students, and the Schocken backlist, strong on education, Kafka, religion, and philosophy, had a good deal of what he needed—but because his tiny store has no stockroom he bought in small quantities.

By midafternoon, we were on the road to Beaumont, Texas, having stopped, just to say hello, at the offices of the L.S.U. Press. The press had several trade books on its list besides Havard's "The Changing Politics of the South"—including a biography of Ellen Glasgow by E. Stanly Godbold, Jr., and "Hugo Black: The Alabama Years," by Virginia Van der Veer Hamilton—and Scheer was able to report that sales had been going reasonably well.

The skies broke open as we entered Beaumont. Scheer had to stop driving for a few minutes; the cascade of water was too much for the windshield wipers. Then it let up slightly, and we turned in at the next motel we came to, a Ramada Inn, where he had not made a reservation. I was surprised, but Scheer explained that he makes reservations at only a few motels on his route, in order to have some mail addresses. "If I made reservations all the way, I'd just have to change them every time I got off schedule, and that would take hours. If I hit a storm like this one, I want to be able to stop. It's tourists who make reservations, because they're afraid of being shut out completely. The motels that cater primarily to travelling salesmen are seldom sold out. When one is, I know another that isn't. On weekends, of course, they're practically empty. Every salesman who can possibly make it has gone streaking for home."

Scheer had to write several letters, fill in the headings on the order forms—the names and addresses of the stores, the dates, the names of the buyers, and the order numbers—and make some long-distance calls. He was putting in two hours of office work a night, usually between ten and midnight, and we were regularly breakfasting at seven-thirty. Yet, as far as I could tell, Scheer was thriving on his seventeen- or eighteen-hour days. "It's true," he said. "I am exhilarated by it. I suppose it does not really seem like work to me. It takes a lot of energy, but I don't notice that unless I get sick on a trip. I have to laugh, though, when people ask, 'What is there to do at night?' As you have seen, I work at night, when I am not having dinner with friends. As I recall, I've been to the movies on the road twice in the past ten years."

Scheer had only two calls to make in Beaumont the next day, Thursday. He called on Reta Piland, head librarian of the Jefferson County Library—a most unusual account. Libraries seldom buy from trade-book salesmen; rather, they rely on institutional jobbers or specialized school, university, and institutional salesmen. Mrs. Piland ordered a lot of titles, and, because she was buying for a main library and three branch libraries, in most cases she thought of four copies almost as one.

At the Key Book Shop, our other planned stop in Beaumont, Scheer was told that Tom Clemmons, the owner, was out to lunch. He took the news philosophically. It is a small store, heavily slanted toward best-sellers and popular nonfiction, and Scheer introduced himself to the salesgirl (the first time on our trip that he had had to introduce himself), chatted with her about what he discovered was her home town—Boston—and, while he talked, went through a set of his catalogues, marking a title here and a title there, perhaps twenty-five or thirty in all. He handed the marked catalogues to the girl. "Give Tom my best, and tell him I'm sorry to miss seeing him," he said. "I'd wait, but I've got to move on to Houston. And Tom needn't worry. I've marked everything he'll want to consider." With that, we were gone. The call had taken not more than twenty minutes.

As we drove, Scheer told me that ordinarily he counts marking the catalogues, the way he had just done, as a poor substitute for selling but that this case was not so bad. "Tom Clemmons really does not want to hear what I have to say about the books," he explained. "He just wants to know which books will be advertised or listed in *Book Chat*." Then Scheer realized he had to explain that *Book Chat* is a bimonthy publication, produced in Chicago, that describes eighty or ninety new books in its editorial columns. Local bookstores' names are imprinted on it, and the stores distribute it to their customers; the back cover includes two prepaid tear-out postcards addressed to a particular store, to be used as order forms. "*Book Chat* puts out a huge Christmas issue, and there are several Christmas-gift catalogues of the same sort, imprinted the same way," Scheer said. "They are influential. All my accounts want to know what is going to be in *Book Chat* and the Christmas catalogues. It's something I note in the jacket-book whenever I have the information. How do customers hear about the existence of a new book? It is hard to accept the fact that not everyone reads the *Times Book Review* every week, but we have to face it. People expect their bookseller to tell them what has been published. The bookstore has a news-bearing function. And *Book Chat* is one of the ways it fulfills it."

By late afternoon,

we were in Houston, and Scheer's spirits were effervescent. "Now we're in a real book town," he said. "Houston is a city where I drive seventy-five miles a day inside the city limits and don't ever mind it. No matter how badly a trip may have been going, Houston revives me." Scheer has watched Houston grow, since 1946, from a city he could cover in two days into one that occupies him for at least seven, and sometimes ten. (His second-longest stop, of four or five days, is in Dallas.) He would not be in the least surprised, he said, if within less than a decade Houston rose to fourth place in the ranking of book-buying cities. There was a stack of mail, including a tape cassette from Hawthorn, waiting for Scheer at the Travelodge Motel; Hawthorn, as an experiment, was equipping its salesmen with cassette recorders to facilitate two-way communication with the sales manager. Before he read his letters or listened to the cassette, Scheer was on the telephone talking to Ted Brown, another good friend. At the time, Brown owned two bookstores in Houston: Brown Book Shop, in the heart of the old downtown business district, the best-known bookstore in the Southwest, and Brown's Post Oak, in the Post Oak shopping complex, part of one of the city's several satellite downtowns. (Brown has since opened a third store.) Houston had a hundred and fifty suburban shopping centers at last count, but the Post Oak-Westheimer complex, a glittering expanse of white buildings and gray parking lots just off the vast oval freeway system, is the eye-opener. In addition to

54

Brown's Post Oak, the area includes such attractions as Sakowitz, Neiman-Marcus, and Joske's—all department stores—and the Galleria, which is an enclosed, air-conditioned shopping mall on three levels, with around a hundred shops, an ice-skating rink, an art gallery, and two movie theatres.

Brown told Scheer he was getting ready to close the downtown store for the day but said there was time for us to get there if we hurried, so we hurried. A tall, dapper man with a flamboyant mustache, given to boldly striped shirts, Brown seems to qualify well for Scheer's encomium "a real bookman." He not only loves books but manages his stores with attention to every detail. He presides over the downtown store, like a captain on the bridge of a ship, from a square combination counter and office just inside the plate-glass doors. The store is a big, no-nonsense place with a large stock—rows of books on racks and shelves, many with just their spines visible. It looks cluttered, but Brown, who has thirteen saleswomen and salesmen working for him, knows exactly where every book is. The downtown store is patronized predominantly by men, and stocks a lot of books on business, economics, science, art, and history. (It carries, for instance, all of Samuel Eliot Morison's fifteen-volume "History of United States Naval Operations in World War II.") Brown's Post Oak is more for women, and tidiness is its hallmark; the books are well displayed, and the emphasis is on fiction, cookbooks, and the household arts. Brown has a reputation for being tough on book salesmen. He is uncommonly knowledgeable about books, and art books are a specialty of his. (A salesman once showed him advance proofs of a splendid collection of Picasso's work in which one abstraction was reproduced upside down; Brown recognized the error instantly and was the first to report it to the publisher.) He barks at salesmen who assume that hyperbole will impress him. Since Scheer knows Brown well, he not only refrains from hyperbole but when Brown barks he barks right back.

Brown told us that his wife, Sylvia, who runs the Post Oak store, was there and would not be leaving for a little while, so we drove out to say hello to her—about six miles through a succession of residential districts with names like River Oaks, Tall Timbers, and Afton Oaks. Scheer chatted with Sylvia Brown for a few minutes, and then we drove to another bookstore, named Cobler's Book Store, at Post Oak for a chat with its buyer, Bill Caskey. (Two other places also sell books in the Post Oak-Westheimer area: the book department of Joske's, and the Sam Houston Book Shop, in the Galleria.)

Scheer started selling in earnest the following day. That was Friday, and it was his ambition to finish Houston by the following Thursday, in time to drive the two hundred miles to San Antonio, his next stop, that evening; he could make it if his appointments dropped into place perfectly. Counting the Post Oak-Westheimer area stores, Scheer had thirteen buyers, buying for twenty bookstores, on his list; among his first calls were those on Bill Streich, of Bookland; Brian Sumrall, of Books Incorporated; Jean Ball, of Jean's Book Shoppe; and Jessie Allen, of Allen-Maxwell Books. He hoped if possible, to enlarge the list. He knew of a couple of new stores he had never called on, and if time permitted he wanted at least to scout them out and see whether they were worth adding to his future trips. Scheer's pace through New

Orleans, Baton Rouge, and Beaumont had awed me. It was clear that in Houston he intended to step it up.

At our seven-thirty breakfast on Friday in the motel's dining room, Scheer told me, over enormous glasses of Texas orange juice, that he had been up and working for a couple of hours, answering letters and listening to the Hawthorn cassette. "They gave me a few compliments, but mostly they gave me hell," he said of the message on the cassette. "The sales manager thinks I am not doing well enough with Emily Gardiner Neal's book, 'The Healing Power of Christ'—not as well as his other salesmen, that is. I'm sure he suspects me of skipping some religious bookstores, but I think the whole thing is a misunderstanding. I'm nearly a month behind the rest of the Hawthorn men, and I think—I *hope*—he is comparing my very early figures with their much more complete results. Anyhow, I checked my figures on the Neal up through Beaumont, and they look all right. I know for sure that I have not been skipping the religious bookstores. First chance I get, I'll dictate an up-to-date report, and maybe the sales manager will feel better."

Scheer looked rather distressed, and I asked whether he resented being scolded, especially by a tape recording. His frown immediately changed to a broad smile. "It's quite the other way around," he said. "Naturally, I don't want to be scolded at all, but I could be missing a trick without realizing it. He also asked me what handle I am using on 'Home Landscaping You Can Design Yourself,' so he can pass the word on to the other men. Apparently, my figures on that one are excellent. I admire the way Hawthorn is keeping on top of the sales picture. That's what it should be doing, and its doing it well."

In the course

of the week, Scheer managed to fit in all his accounts. He never stopped if it was at all possible to keep going; Sunday he devoted to writing up orders, writing letters, answering Hawthorn's tape, taking his mail to the main post office, and dining at the Ted Browns'. He was pleased by the orders he got, especially the one from Brown. Scheer guessed that, in all, the orders were about ten per cent bigger, in dollars, than those a year earlier; nearly all the buyers said that their sales were up by about that percentage since then. Scheer also made time before, after, and between his main appointments for quite a little scouting. He looked in on a camping-equipment store on Westbury Square, thinking that it might be interested in stocking a few copies of a Schocken book called "Bushcraft: A Serious Guide to Survival and Camping," by Richard Graves. But the official opening of the shop was a few days off, and a busy young man who was assembling a bright-orange portable tent said he believed that there was a plan to have a shelf of camping books for sale but he wasn't sure. Scheer said he would try to stop by on his next trip. He investigated a wholesaler called Houston Health Food Distributors; two of his new books were "Cooking Creatively with Natural Foods," by Sam and Edith Brown, and "Putting Food By," by Ruth Hertzberg, Beatrice Vaughan, and Janet Greene, and Scheer sold the firm some of these books. If Scheer had an appointment for two o'clock and we had finished lunch by one o'clock, he would remember some place he could go for a quick visit. We stopped at Stelzig Saddlery Company, which sells saddles, boots, guns, and Western hats and clothes. Scheer loves the store, and has stopped there many times before. As a result, it has a small shelf of how-to books about riding and the training of horses. Scheer was worried because his titles did not seem to have been selling well. It was evident to me that Leo Stelzig, Jr., who runs the Saddlery, was not worried, in view of the number of customers who were buying two-hundred-and-seventy-five-dollar boots. Nevertheless, Scheer spent more than an hour in the store. He rearranged the books on the shelf, extracted extra copies of a few titles that needed to be returned, and told Stelzig he had a few new books that belonged in the inventory. Stelzig was happy to go along with whatever Scheer suggested. Then Scheer helped Stelzig carry the returns to the Saddlery shipping room and pack them in cardboard cartons. For lack of other packing-case filler—at least, there was none right at hand—Stelzig filled in the crevices with scraps of high-grade woolly sheepskin, of the kind used to line Stelzig saddles. I wondered what the publishers' warehousemen would think when they opened the cartons. "Of course, spending all that time did not make sense," Scheer said as we drove out of the Saddlery parking lot. "Even if Stelzig's book department quadrupled in size—which, obviously, it is not likely to do— I should not have stayed so long. But if I had to think I couldn't afford a little foolishness, I'd prefer to give up the whole thing. I like talking to Leo Stelzig, and his store delights me. On top of that—my fatal weakness, I suppose—the thought that I may be able to sell three more copies of one of my books, say, 'The Cowboy Trade,' by Glen Rounds, is catnip to the old cat."

On Wednesday, I had to leave Scheer, in order to keep an appointment in New York. By Tuesday night, he was so confident of finishing Houston on time that he had decided to drive down to the Manned Spacecraft Center, thirty-two miles southeast of town, to see friends who had no connection at all with books—former colleagues of Julian Scheer, his younger brother, who had spent nine years as the assistant administrator for public affairs of NASA. Scheer and I had dinner at a Steak & Ale restaurant. "I do wish you could see San Antonio," Scheer said. "It doesn't have Houston's razzle-dazzle—this marvelous mixture of sophistication with the frontier conviction that everything is possible—but San Antonio, I suppose, is even more colorful, in an entirely different way. And it's interesting from a book point of view. I have two big quality-paperback accounts there—retailers with chains of paperback stores—a department store, three or four nice personal bookshops, and two truly fine old-time bookstores."

Scheer remarked that under the expansive Houston skies it was hard to realize that some of the handsome, well-arranged, busy bookstores we had been visiting were operating on the thinnest of economic margins. "They are no different from bookstores everywhere else," he said. "They don't know for sure whether they will wind up in the red or the black for the year until the Christmas rush is over. Christmas saves them, ordinarily. They may do a third of their annual business, or more, in November and December. There have never been as many bookstores in Houston as there are now, but there have been too many failures along the way.

"When any small business is trimmed close," Scheer said,

"and every nickel and dime counts, there is no room for a mistake. A busy bookstore may gross a hundred thousand a year. That means it has to have space for a thirty- or thirty-five-thousand-dollar inventory—say, eight to ten thousand books. A bookstore selling a half-million dollars' worth of books is a landmark, known all over the state. Ted Brown won't tell what his gross is—it's even bigger than that—and, at least within the trade, Brown is famous all over the country. But say you are selling that hundred thousand dollars' worth of books, taking advantage of every strategy and getting maximum discounts. You are paying only some sixty-two to sixty-four thousand dollars for your books, including postage, so ostensibly you have a thirty-six-to-thirty-eight-thousand-dollar profit. But you have to have at least one clerk. You also need a high-school boy who can come in during the late afternoons to help you move the newly arrived book cartons and open them. There's the rent, upkeep, and electricity— and in Houston, at least, you must be air-conditioned. If you buy wisely, your shipping charges on returns will not be much more than a few hundred dollars for the year. And so, if your accountant does not charge too much, and if you refrain from spending too heavily on local advertising, if your insurance isn't too expensive, and if pilferage doesn't run too high, and if almost all of your charge-account customers pay their bills, then it is possible —just possible—that you may have fifteen or sixteen thousand dollars left before taxes. Of course, you have not taken any salary for yourself. But that is the ideal. The real bookseller makes mistakes, all down the line. An accident of any kind— a couple of small robberies, say—can break his back. He does not have the financial strength to survive a serious reversal of any kind. And so you find hundreds of towns big enough to support a bookstore that don't have any. When one went broke, nobody was foolish enough to start another. When a bookstore closes, the book business it was generating often seems to evaporate—it's like the circulation of a newspaper that folds. Where does that business go? Some of it may go miles and miles away—the town's book addicts may drive ninety miles, on Saturday afternoons, to pick up an armful of books at some place like Ted Brown's. Some of it goes to the Book-of-the-Month Club, or another mail-order source. Most of it, I'm convinced, just stops. People quit reading books and turn on television, because they do not have a bookseller who can inspire them to read by telling them what there is to read and by making books seem valuable and exciting and fashionable.

"It takes both talent and industry to operate a successful bookshop. There are people, fortunately, who have enough of both. And an adroit bookseller can make a good living for a lifetime, in a joyous occupation. I do think publishers need to help bookstores in every possible way. It's crucial. Nobody else does what the dedicated bookseller does. Trade publishing must have outlets for good trade books, and to have them it has to give those outlets support.

"For my own part, as a liaison between my publishers and my bookstores, I like to think I'm helping to keep the bookstores alive and healthy—a contribution, in a small way, to the survival of American letters."

About the Author

Bruce Bliven, Jr., a New Yorker who was born in California in 1916, has been a writer by profession since he was graduated from Harvard in 1937. (Bliven, Jr. should not be, but frequently is, confused with his father, who edited *The New Republic* for twenty-five years.) He began as a newspaperman (The Manchester *Guardian*, the New York *Post*), and, since the end of the Second World War, he has contributed articles to a host of national magazines, including *The New Yorker* where "Book Traveller" first appeared. Bliven, Jr. is also the author or coauthor of eight books.